Original title:
The Ocean's Secret Dance

Copyright © 2025 Creative Arts Management OÜ
All rights reserved.

Author: Helena Marchant
ISBN HARDBACK: 978-1-80587-365-5
ISBN PAPERBACK: 978-1-80587-835-3

## Whirl of Seafoam and Heartbeats

The sea foam hops like beans,
It juggles fish with silly dreams.
A crab in boots is quite a sight,
While seaweed dances, feeling light.

Gull calls out with a witty quip,
As dolphins glide with a playful dip.
The surfboards giggle as they chase,
The tiny waves in a frothy race.

## The Dancer Beneath the Surface

Bubbles rise with winks and grins,
As mermaids twirl in fins with spins.
They throw a party, oh so grand,
With coral snacks and seaweed bands.

Turtles shuffle, doing the crab,
While octopuses try to jab.
A clam forgot its dance routine,
And looks quite puzzled, poor little bean.

## Waves Crashing in Soliloquy

The waves talk loudly, full of sass,
As shells roll over, oh what a class.
They argue who's the biggest splash,
While starfish watch and start to laugh.

With every crash, a funny tale,
Of fish that danced within the gale.
"Did you see that?" the tide demands,
As sea cucumbers wave their hands.

## Whispers of the Tide's Embrace

Coral giggles, a cheeky tease,
As sea horses waltz with the breeze.
"Who's got the best moves?" asks a ray,
While little shrimps just dance away.

The currents swirl, a frothy jest,
As spotted fish engage in quest.
With each soft sigh, the water sings,
Of joyful jumps and silly flings.

## Choreography of the Brackish Waters

In the shallows, fish take flight,
With a twist and a playful bite.
Squids wear ties for a fancy glance,
As clams join in the merry dance.

Octopus twirls in wobbly style,
While crabs shuffle with a cheeky smile.
Seaweed sways in a leafy spree,
Bubbles giggle, oh so carefree.

## Rhythms Unveiled by the Moon's Glow

Underneath, where shadows play,
Starfish waltz in a bright ballet.
"You call that a dip?" says one to two,
A lobster spins, just to make stew.

Walrus tries a breakdance move,
But penguins laugh, as he can't groove.
They slip and slide, quite nonchalant,
With laughter echoing, a funny haunt.

## Whispers of the Deep

Eels wiggle with a pep in their tail,
While turtles plot to set their own sail.
"Catch me if you can!" one fish will tease,
As jellyfish float like inflatable cheese.

A crab's a prince, with a crown made of sand,
Fetch me a drink, that's his highest demand.
While sea urchins grumble, stuck in their shell,
They quite enjoy their quirky hotel.

## **Tides of the Hidden Realm**

Mollusks groove on their slippery stage,
Ballet tights sewn from a foamy page.
A starfish kicks off, twirling around,
Drawing laughter from all in the sound.

With waves clapping to the seafood beats,
Dolphins dive down, no sign of defeat.
A conch shell sings, making giggles explode,
As bubbles pop out, they seem so bestowed.

## The Fluidity of Forgotten Whispers

Waves waltz with the slippery fish,
Crabs cha-cha in their silly dish.
Seashells giggle, sharing a jest,
While seahorses twirl in their best dress.

Jellyfish float with a jelly laugh,
Octopus plays with his squiggly math.
Starfish can't grasp, they just sit tight,
Dreaming of goodies in the moonlight.

## A Dance Beneath the Surface

Bubbles rise like tiny balloons,
As clams groan in their rickety tunes.
Cuddly otters spin round and round,
While sea cucumbers don't make a sound.

Gazing seaweed sways in delight,
Wiggling about, such a funny sight.
With fish playing tag, losing their way,
As laughter echoes, by the bay.

**Eternal Surprises in Submersion**

Mermaids giggle, brushing their hair,
With dolphins leaping without a care.
Turtles bumble, slow but spry,
While plankton boogie, oh my, oh my!

Electric eels add a zap to the beat,
Dancing crabs take the floor with their feet.
Anemones wave with a wave and a grin,
Swaying along like they're in a spin.

## The Hidden Act of the Marine

In the shadows, funny fish play games,
Creating laughter with all their claims.
Eels make faces, with a twist and a pout,
While clowns fish know what fun's all about.

Barnacles juggle, quite the delight,
As lobsters crab-walk under the light.
The sand whispers tales of sly little pranks,
In this deep blue home, where laughter tanks.

## **Lullabies of the Sea's Heart**

The fish wear hats, oh what a sight,
As seaweed sways in the moon's soft light.
Crabs dance jigs on the sandy floor,
While dolphins giggle, always wanting more.

Starfish throw confetti, a colorful show,
Turtles doing limbo, with a graceful flow.
The clams clap along, with a glimmering cheer,
As waves play percussion, loud and clear.

## **Twilight Trysts of the Seabed**

Under a shell, two shrimps hold hands,
Planning a party where everyone stands.
Octopuses juggle, with a smile so wide,
While seahorses twirl, taking life in stride.

Mussels sing in harmony, tones so refined,
Happily searching for pearls that shine.
A blowfish in bowtie, such dapper flair,
Spins tales of adventure from his clammy lair.

## Harmonies of the Briny Depths

The jellyfish waltz, in their polka-dot best,
While minnows create bubbles, it's all a jest.
A narwhal's serenade floats through the waves,
As creatures below plot their next silly raves.

Eels with a mohawk, strut with style,
Flipping their tails, all the while.
The barnacles cheer, they're most impressed,
Donning tiny tuxedos, they join the fest.

## Sonorous Beats of the Coast

Crabs with drumsticks make a raucous beat,
While the sand grins softly beneath their feet.
Clams whistle tunes, they're quite the show,
And fish on a trampoline, bouncing below.

The gulls pull pranks, swooping low,
Daring the sea anemones to put on a show.
As the tide rolls in, the laughter grows loud,
Mixing sea foam with joy, all are proud.

### **Beneath the Turquoise Veil**

In the depths where fish wear shoes,
They hold dance parties with seaweed blues.
Octopuses juggle pearls with flair,
Crabs tap dance without a care.

The starfish play the tambourine,
While scallops wink, looking so keen.
Clams clap along in gleeful cheer,
Who knew the deep could be so dear?

## Melodies in salt and foam

A dolphin sings a silly song,
While jellyfish bounce the night along.
Seahorses glide, dressed to impress,
Doing ballet in their flowing dress.

The eels hum tunes, oh what a sight,
As they groove to the rhythm, left and right.
With bubbles popping, they share a joke,
Creating laughter with every poke.

## The Silent Waltz of the Abyss

In shadows deep, where laughter hides,
A squid spins tales on tiny rides.
With a wink and a squirt, it steals the scene,
Its ink reveals a colorful sheen.

The turtles nod, with shells that shine,
Digging grooves in the ocean brine.
They whisper secrets, oh so sly,
Of dance-offs where the jellyfish fly.

## **Currents of Enchanted Waters**

The fish wear hats and have tea breaks,
Crooning softly while the coral shakes.
Otters slide down on a sparkling wave,
Bringing giggles that the otters crave.

The sea cucumbers explore the floor,
Finding treasures that they adore.
They shimmy and shake with all their might,
A splash of fun in the soft moonlight.

## Hidden Crescendo of the Sea

In the depths, where fish do prance,
Tiny bubbles start to dance.
Seaweed sways in joyful glee,
Whispers shared 'tween fishy spree.

Octopus plays a sneaky game,
Stealing sunglasses, oh what shame!
Dolphins leap with cheesy grins,
While crabs prepare for water spins.

A conch shell boasts its tales so grand,
Telling stories of sea and sand.
With every wave, laughter echoes,
As jellyfish float in daring shows.

In this realm of bubbles and swirls,
Sea creatures giggle, flip, and twirl.
An underwater symphony bright,
Fins and tails in pure delight.

## **Fish Scales and Stardust**

Fish in bow ties swim with flair,
Crabs in hats, a sight so rare.
Starfish hold a disco ball,
While sea cucumbers try to crawl.

The clownfish jokes, a swim so bold,
Telling tales of treasure gold.
A shrimp prepares for limbo night,
Under the beams of soft moonlight.

Pufferfish puff, trying to hide,
With a wink, he takes in stride.
Seahorses trot in high design,
Donning pearls, looking divine.

In this watery world so bright,
Where shrimp can dance and fish take flight.
Giggles ripple beneath the sea,
Where every wave holds joy and glee.

## The Dance of Dune and Wave

Waves shimmy, a frothy surprise,
While seagulls wear their sunblock guise.
Sandcastles sway in the breezy air,
With crabs playing king, no need to share.

The tide pulls back with a whoosh and sway,
Tickling toes, come join the play!
A fish flips up with a silly grin,
As sea stars cheer him to win.

Shells rattle as if they can talk,
While the dolphins teach a funky walk.
Ocean's humor drips like rain,
In this paradise, who feels pain?

The beach, a stage for a grand parade,
With each wave, new games are played.
Sand and surf in light ballet,
A rollicking show, hip, hip hooray!

## Echoes of Time in Aquatic Dreams

In the depths, echoes giggle and play,
As sea turtles waltz with their ballet.
Old shipwrecks laugh with rusty pride,
While fish chase memories, side by side.

Mermaids compete in a whimsical race,
With clam shells on their faces, what a case!
Urchins shoot confetti from their lairs,
As whales hum tunes that ripple through layers.

A jellyfish breezes with a fancy sway,
Lighting up the night in a dazzling display.
Starry-eyed kids at the surface glance,
Caught in the magic of a watery dance.

In currents where laughter and dreams collide,
Time slips away with the joyful tide.
Echoes of fun, sound sweet and grand,
In the aquatic realm, wonder's on hand.

## **The Saltwater's Hidden Mambo**

Fish in tuxedos twirl with grace,
Crabs in high hats join the race.
Jellyfish jiggle, what a sight!
They cha-cha near the moonlit light.

Starfish clap their hands so bright,
While dolphins giggle in pure delight.
Seagulls squawk a silly tune,
As waves make love beneath the moon.

Barnacles groove on rocks all day,
While octopuses play hide and sway.
The reef throws a wild underwater bash,
And the sand dollars dance with a splash!

Mermaids laugh and flip their hair,
With sea turtles spinning without a care.
Pull up a shell and join the fun,
In the ocean's dance, there's room for everyone!

## Breath of the Lapping Rhythms

Gentle waves whisper silly pranks,
As seaweed sways and giggles in ranks.
Starfish shout, "Catch me if you can!"
While crabs scuttle, they're part of the plan.

Sandy toes and splashes galore,
Even the jellyfish are hard to ignore.
They twirl and twist in their bubbly show,
With a wink and a wave, they steal the flow.

Seashells gossip beneath the sun,
Shellfish giggle, oh, what fun!
Anchor's up, it's wild and zany,
As fish parade, all bright and brainy!

From dolphin dives to big whale grins,
The pulse of the deep always spins.
And in every splash and playful move,
Lies a rhythm that makes you groove!

## Sailing with the Depth's Secrets

A ship sails forth with a silly crew,
Pirates in hats, what a motley view!
They trade jokes with every gust,
Hoping to find treasure or just some crust.

The parrot squawks like it's in a play,
While sailors dance the night away.
Hoisting sails with laughter loud,
While fish cheer on the merry crowd.

A kraken serves as DJ, oh so sly,
With tentacles waving, reaching for the sky.
Mermaid backup dancers in the sea,
Groovin' to rhythms, wild and free!

With each wave that comes to play,
The ship bobs up in the climbing spray.
Who knew deep waters held such jest?
In the heart of the depths, we're truly blessed!

# The Unfolding of Tidal Tales

Every tide brings a tale untold,
Of fish in gowns and seaweed bold.
A clam performed a duet with glee,
And a crab played tambourine on a tree!

Listening closely, hear them chirp,
As dolphins leap and seahorses burp.
The ebbs and flows a quirky band,
With sea foam frolicking upon the sand.

Tidal waves do a wiggly dance,
Organs of shells near the fools in a trance.
Stories swirl in salty air,
With each splash, a giggle to share!

Octopus whispers secrets to the gull,
While fishy robots spin and twirl.
So come take a plunge, join the fun,
In the ocean's jest, we're never done!

## **The Unseen Ballet of the Surf**

Waves in tutus leap and spin,
Clowns in the sea, they dive right in.
Seagulls giggle, doing their tricks,
As fish form a line for a seaweed fix.

Starfish clapping with their five hands,
While crabs perform in the sandy bands.
Water spins like a soggy top,
Under the sun, they never stop.

Shells wearing hats laugh at the tide,
In this watery show, there's nothing to hide.
The sand joins the dance, tap-tapping away,
As the moon sets the stage for another big play.

So join in the fun, let your worries float,
Dance to the rhythm of this silly boat.
With bubbles as confetti flying high,
Who knew sea life could be such a guy?

## Echoing Secrets of the Deep Blue

Whales play hide and seek in the swell,
With bubble-blowing tricks, they cast quite a spell.
The jellyfish jiggle with glee, so bright,
While squids squirt ink, oh, what a sight!

Crabs in sneakers dance on the sand,
Wiggling their claws like they've got a band.
Anemones sway, like they've got the moves,
In the depths of the blue, where the sea life grooves.

Eels with swagger, all dressed to impress,
Sliding and gliding, they'll never say less.
Barnacles gossip about the beach folk,
While shells tell tall tales - oh what a joke!

The ocean's a stage, funny creatures abound,
Each wave is a laugh, a comic rebound.
So let's splash along, share a giggle or two,
In this wild underwater hullabaloo!

## The Fluid Dynamics of Dreams

Bubbles like balloons float past my face,
Frogs pretending they're in a race.
Sea cucumbers crawl with grace and pride,
While dolphins wiggle, their joy cannot hide.

Horseshoe crabs tapping their rhythm on rocks,
With octopuses painting - what a paradox!
The tide rolls in with a chuckle and sway,
As kelp gets tangled, and decided to play.

Turtles in glasses reading old maps,
Finding lost treasure - oh, the silly mishaps!
Flounders floundering in their own parade,
Laughing at fish who forgot why they strayed.

So join in this comedy, a tide of surprise,
Dreams take a dip just beneath the skies.
With every splash, a giggle unfurls,
In the dance of the sea, where humor twirls!

## Secrets in the Foam

Foamy whispers tickle the shore,
With secrets only the sea can store.
Gulls exchange gossip about the best bait,
While clams are giddy - oh isn't it great?

Dolphins giggling, dodging the swells,
Telling fish tales, casting their spells.
The foam erupts like a bubbly cheer,
While sea stars giggle, come gather near.

An underwater concert of fin and scale,
With crabs on stage, and lobsters to hail.
The squishy sea sponge softens the fall,
In a world where silliness answers the call.

Let's dance with the tide, find joy in the spray,
Every droplet a chuckle, the salt leads the way.
With glee in our hearts, we surf the wild seas,
Unlocking the laughter with every breeze!

**The Rhythm of Submerged Repose**

Bubbles giggle, fish take flight,
A clam's got jokes, what a sight!
Octopus jives with a fancy flair,
While seahorses twirl without a care.

Crabs tap dance on the ocean floor,
Shells are clapping, give them more!
Starfish try to catch the beat,
With every wave, they shuffle their feet.

A dolphin dives in a playful spin,
Whales hum softly, let the fun begin!
Coral sways as if it knows,
How to laugh when the tidal flow goes.

So join the fun, it's quite absurd,
Underwater laughter, haven't you heard?
With each splash, a smile awaits,
In this blue realm, joy radiates!

## Unveiling the Water's Veil

Anemones wave with a cheeky grin,
While shy little eels peek out, then in.
Puffers puff up, trying to impress,
With silly poses, they'll never confess.

Turtles glide, like an old, wise sage,
With a wink that suggests a hidden page.
Jellyfish jiggle, a wobbly dance,
In their own world, they take a chance.

Fish gossip low, in whispers and giggles,
About the mermaid who occasionally wiggles.
A treasure chest filled with clams and pearls,
Is just a spot for yet more swirls.

So let the waves bring forth the cheer,
As the sea reveals laughter crystal clear.
With every tide, the joy does swell,
In this watery realm, all is well!

## Secrets Entwined in Seaweed

Tangled seaweed, a fabulous mess,
Where fish love to hide, and crabs wear a dress.
Little shrimps dance on a floating branch,
While jellyfish giggle, lost in their trance.

Starfish spin, trying to be sly,
As seagulls squawk "oh my, oh my!"
A treasure of socks, in a shipwrecked trunk,
Brings hugs from the dolphins, in playful junk.

The octopus whispers a riddle or two,
While plankton disco under skies of blue.
Barnacles clap as they stick around,
In this underwater humor, joy is found.

So swish and sway with the tides that flow,
In the lead and the follow, just let go!
For in the depth, where secrets are brewed,
Lives the essence of laughter, never subdued!

## Oceanic Dreams and Dance

Swirling currents, a dance divine,
Where dolphins leap and rays entwine.
A mermaid twirls with a sequined tail,
As bubbles explode in a giggling trail.

Fish form a line for a conga jam,
While the sea turtles cheer, "Oh, what a fam!"
A playful squid sketches designs in the sand,
Creating fun shapes that look quite grand.

Glimmers of sunlight bounce and play,
Turning the waves into glittering sway.
A sandcastle busts out with a dragon's roar,
As seagulls dive in, looking for more!

So let's ride the wave of silliness bold,
Where laughter and joy in blue waters unfold.
In this magical realm where dreams take flight,
We dance and we play—what a sheer delight!

## **Melodies from the Maritime Depths**

Bubbles rise with a giggle,
Fish wear hats that wiggle.
Crabs tap dance on the floor,
While jellyfish float and explore.

Turtles giggle in their shells,
Sailors shout, 'Who rang the bells?'
Octopuses fashion a band,
With seaweed strings, oh so grand!

Starfish spin in a conga line,
Seagulls giggle, feeling fine.
The waves clap, a jolly crew,
As dolphins join in, just for you!

So dive deep, don't be shy,
Join the fun where fish dance by.
With each splash, joy found anew,
Marine antics waiting for you!

## **Secrets in the Sea Breeze**

Whispers float on salty air,
Where mermaids braid their sunny hair.
Seashells gossip as they lie,
Oh, that nautilus, such a sly guy!

Crabby tales of shipwrecked dreams,
Dance with laughter, burst at the seams.
Fishes tell their jokes so bright,
Tickling waves, oh what a sight!

Seagulls squawk in playful squabbles,
Plotting pranks and ocean bobbles.
A clam might wink, a fish might pout,
Join us now, let laughter out!

So breathe in deep, the breeze calls you,
To secrets shared by the ocean's crew.
With each chuckle, the sea's delight,
Brings a smile from morn till night!

## The Song of Shifting Sands

Grains of gold, they sing and sway,
Tickling toes that come to play.
A starfish strums a sandy tune,
While crabs dance 'neath the watchful moon.

Seashells form a clever band,
With seaweed drapes, they take a stand.
Footprints tell a goofy tale,
As wind-turned whispers swirl and wail.

Surfboards flip in a frothy laugh,
As dolphins trot in a splashy half.
The tide curtsies, bows with glee,
Come join the jolly jamboree!

In shifting sands, the jokes abound,
With every swell, new fun is found.
So dance along with a happy heart,
In the sandy playground, be a part!

## Dance of Shadows in Salty Waters

Fish in tuxedos glide with grace,
Casting shadows, what a chase!
Lobsters do a silly jig,
While plankton twirls, oh so big!

Waves get frisky, jump and dive,
Making sure the fun's alive.
Seahorses waltz in pairs so neat,
While the sun sets, oh what a treat!

Sardines swirl in a shimmery dance,
Bringing giggles with each chance.
The moon hums a lullaby tune,
As the night blooms, laugh like a loon!

So dive into this light-hearted spree,
Where shadows tango in salty glee.
Let the ocean's humor abound,
In every splash, joy is found!

## Fluid Poetry of the Tide

Waves that wiggle, splash, and sway,
Fish throw parties at the bay,
Seagulls laugh in silly flight,
While crabs tap dance in moonlight.

Surfboards wobble, riders frown,
As seaweed weaves a gown of brown,
Salty breezes blow with glee,
Tickling toes of you and me.

Shells are shuffling on the shore,
Whispers of tides that ask for more,
They twirl and twist beneath the foam,
Each ripple finds a place called home.

Jellyfish do their jiggly jig,
While octopuses play peek-a-boo big,
Underwater giggles, bubbles burst,
In the deep, they quench their thirst.

## **Veiled Movements of the Marine**

Under seaweed, secrets hide,
Fish in masks host a wild ride,
Turtles tumble through the blue,
While sea cucumbers wiggle too.

Starfish sneak in silly games,
Playing tag with funny names,
Crabby dancers steal the show,
As mermaids casually row.

Whales hum tunes that make us grin,
While dolphins playfully spin,
Dancing shadows, light-hearted winks,
As the tide flows, the ocean thinks.

Barnacles rock in their own way,
To the rhythm of a salty ballet,
With every splash, laughter sings,
And the sea keeps all its flings.

## Chorus of the Whispering Waters

Laughter bubbles from the deep,
As fish gossip secrets to keep,
Clams clap shells in rhythmic cheer,
While sea sponges whisper near.

Waves engage in cheeky fights,
Spraying spouts with watery bites,
Gulls drop jokes from aloft,
As seashells roll, oh, so soft.

Eels slide slick with giggly grace,
And sea stars wear smiles on each face,
Bubbles float with tales galore,
In a chorus that begs for more.

Even the rocks start to sway,
As sea urchins join the play,
With each splash, a giggly tune,
The ocean sparkles like a cartoon.

## Currents of the Unseen

Currents swirl and whirl around,
Sharing secrets, laughter's sound,
Fish in tuxedos prance about,
While lazy waves simply pout.

Seashells telling jokes so loud,
Dancing 'neath a leafy shroud,
They clack and tap in merry glee,
While rays of sun sip salty tea.

Wobbly turtles in a race,
Pumpkin-colored crabs find their place,
Whimsical dance with fins displayed,
In this vibrant masquerade.

Floppy seals who juggle fish,
With every flip, they grant a wish,
The ocean's pulse, a fun refrain,
Sings of joy through salt and rain.

## Whispers Beneath the Waves

Fish wearing hats, what a sight,
They giggle and wiggle, oh what delight!
Crabs in pajamas, strutting with flair,
They dance in the currents without a care.

Octopus playing chess with a seal,
The king's pawn dashed, it's quite the deal.
Jellyfish juggling their own little lights,
While dolphins are debating the best kite flights.

Seaweed swaying, like it's on a spree,
Kelp getting jealous of the limelight, you see?
They argue the style of a good ocean twist,
But all just wave and can't be missed!

So next time you dive, take a good glance,
You might see fish giving the ocean a chance.
In the deep blue, a riot unfolds,
With laughter and joy, more precious than gold.

## Crystalline Echoes of the Deep

Bubbles rising, they whisper sweet tales,
Of turtles who dream of fantastic gales.
Clams have the gossip, oh don't they know?
Secretly shelling out stories in tow.

Starfish playing tag on the sandy floor,
While sea anemones open their door.
With fins all a-flutter and shells all aglow,
They've got the moves that surely steal the show.

A walrus reciting his favorite joke,
As sharks are just laughing, not trying to poke!
Mermaids in chorus, their giggles abound,
Echoing softly through waters profound.

So come take a peek, but keep it discreet,
These underwater mischief-makers can't be beat.
In layers of laughter, the antics don't cease,
In this watery world, hilarity's a feast.

## **Tides of Hidden Rhythms**

Sea cucumbers grooving to music unheard,
With jellies doing somersaults, isn't that absurd?
A crab moonwalks, showing off his best tricks,
While sea urchins poke fun with their needle-like picks.

Dolphins in disco, with flair and style,
Grooving along, they can dance for a mile.
Clownfish joke around in their anemone cave,
Declaring it's the best party they can wave!

An octopus DJ, spinning shells with great glee,
Twirling beats through the depths, too wild to see.
Barnacles tapping their feet to the tune,
While a grouper sings softly, under the moon.

So tide on in, where fun bubbles high,
With splashes of laughter beneath the big sky.
For in these deep waters, where silliness flows,
The rhythms of joy always beckon and grows.

## Dance of the Siren's Song

A siren in slippers tries out a jig,
With puffers and triggers, they clear out the fig.
Makes waves in her wake, a splash quite absurd,
As seahorses giggle and mock the old bird.

Mermaids serenading with hairbrushes bright,
Chorus of sea life, shining in light.
Whales swap stories and laugh till they're blue,
Telling tall tales of fish that they knew.

A turtle behind her, swaying slow,
Swapping out dance moves with flair and flow.
Fish twist and shimmy, a flock full of cheer,
With bubbles of laughter, they dance without fear.

So come join the splash in the sparkling foam,
Where laughter and rhythm create a bright home.
In the depths of the sea, joy shines bright and strong,
In each wave, each ripple, a whimsical song.

## Dance of Selkie and Siren

In a seaweed swirl, they twirl around,
Selkie and Siren, both lost and found.
One's got a fish tail, the other's just scales,
Together they giggle, sharing their tales.

With a flip and a flop, they compete for the prize,
Who can catch sea foam with the best of their tries?
Selkie dives low, while Siren sings high,
Their laughter erupts like the gulls in the sky.

Tangled in bubbles, they stumble and glide,
In this watery waltz, there's nowhere to hide.
Though the sea's a bit salty, they don't mind the taste,
As they splash through the waves in a merry-old haste.

With a wink and a splash, they plan a new trick,
Each ripple and wave makes them dance even quick.
In a swirl of the tides, they keep spinning 'round,
In this maritime ballet, true joy can be found.

## Melodies of the Tranquil Abyss

Beneath the waves, where the sea creatures hum,
Floppy fish disco, they shake and they thrum.
With each little bubble, the beat starts to sway,
In a soft, mellow tide, they dance night and day.

Octopus bop with eight silly limbs,
Trying to show off, but they're losing their whims.
Fish flash a smile, as they glide on by,
"Don't take it too seriously," says a shimmering guy.

Seahorses glide, in their fanciest suits,
Flipping and flopping in their tiny root boots.
Kelp gives a shimmy, swaying to the sound,
While a kraken chuckles, lost in the round.

So gather around for the groove of the deep,
Where laughter and bubbles are all that we keep.
In this hidden disco, we all take a chance,
Finding joy in the depths with each silly dance.

## Oceanic Terpsichore

Whales in tuxedos, ready to sway,
Ballet in blue, what a sight to display!
They leap and they twirl with such grand finesse,
As dolphins throw parties in playful excess.

Turtles in ties, doing waltzes so slow,
While clownfish chuckle, "Let's put on a show!"
The crabs join in with their pinch and their clap,
Creating a rhythm on this oceanic map.

With jellyfish lanterns glowing so bright,
They turn the sea floor into pure delight.
Each fin and each flipper, all join in the fun,
Until morning arrives, and the ocean's undone.

So here's to the dance in the waves and the breeze,
Where laughter and music is all we need, please.
In this watery gala, come join the parade,
For life is a dance, in this splashy charade.

## Glistening Rhythms of the Rolling Sea

The surf starts to giggle, the tide starts to tease,
With a light-hearted jig in the warm summer breeze.
Seabirds croon tunes from their lofty high peaks,
While sand dollars tap dance in little sea creeks.

Crabs in cool shades, doing their moves,
With a shuffle and scuttle, they find all their grooves.
The starfish just winks, as they watch from the floor,
Saying, "Join the bash, don't be such a bore!"

In the crash of the waves, there's a chorus so bright,
As shells lend a hand, drumming soft through the night.
With each sparkling ripple, joy fills the air,
A sea-side serenade, nothing can compare.

So let's dance together, in this whimsical scene,
No need for a reason, just let go and glean.
With each twist and turn, feel the rhythm set free,
As we all sync our hearts to the rolling sea.

## Mystical Whirl of the Waves

Waves tickle toes like playful cats,
Spraying salty laughs at silly hats.
Fish wear bow ties, they swim in style,
Crabs tap dance, go ahead and smile.

Seagulls gossip, flap their wings wide,
Sharing secrets they just can't hide.
Starfish gossip with a wink and a grin,
"Who's got the best moves? Come join in!"

Barnacles giggle, stuck on their rock,
"Watch our moves, we really can shock!"
Squid swirl around in a colorful spree,
Twisting and turning, so wild and free.

So come take a dip, let's all take a chance,
In the splashy humor of this water dance.
Wave your arms, don't hold back a cheer,
In this silly party, there's nothing to fear!

## The Dance of Shells and Shadows

Shells on the shore, they shimmy and slide,
With old wise crabs as the stars of their ride.
Jellyfish waltz with a gelatin flare,
While clams clap their pearls, add a touch of flair.

Seaweed sways in a zany ballet,
Tangled in laughter, they sway and they play.
Fiddler crabs bring their tiny drum beat,
As the tide keeps the rhythm so light on their feet.

The shadows of fish have a twisty design,
Joking with sea cucumbers, making them shine.
Barnacle buddies join in a row,
As laughter erupts, stealing the show.

Seagulls act silly, let loose with a caw,
They jump in the waves with a comical flaw.
All in good fun, together we'll prance,
In this watery realm, let's dance and enhance!

## Whirling Secrets of the Undercurrent

Bubbles talk secrets as they rise up high,
Whispers of jellyfish float by implying,
"Did you see Gary, he twirled like a pro?"
Splashing and giggling, putting on a show!

Octopus over here piled high with flair,
A polka-dotted suit, no need to compare.
He does backflips, then bubbles with pride,
While fish try to follow, losing their glide.

The eels do a conga, swaying their tails,
Manta rays glide, sharing silly tales.
Starfish hold hands, arms all intertwined,
In this underwater party, no one is blind!

Crabby comedians cracking up the crowd,
As they shuffle and joke, feeling quite proud.
In this wiggly whirl, let laughter ignite,
For the secrets of currents are pure delight!

## Enchanted Waters' Waltz

Seashells spin like tops in the sand,
Sand dollars watching, all part of the band.
Waves roll and tumble, laughing on the shore,
As dolphins leap high with a splash and a roar.

A sea turtle twirls with grace and finesse,
While clownfish giggle in their zany dress.
Starfish strut with a flair so grand,
In this watery realm, they make a bold stand.

Waves clap together in a cheerful brigade,
As seahorses bob with their bright masquerade.
With every splash, every twist and each turn,
Underwater parties leave us yearning to learn.

So come to the ball where the currents do play,
Join in the fun, take a dip, and sway!
Beneath the moonlight, it's a watery trance,
Dive in, shake it up, don't miss this chance!

## A Symphony of Blue Shadows

Waves do the cha-cha in sunlit glee,
Bubbles pop like corks, just wait and see.
Fish wear glasses and dance on the flake,
Seagulls squawk lyrics, for goodness' sake!

Crabs on the sand kick their tiny shoes,
Shells spin and twirl in colorful hues.
Starfish do cartwheels with elegant flair,
The sea's a circus with naught a care!

Jellyfish wobble like wobbly jigs,
Sand dollars sip tea with their fancy digs.
Surfboards are flying, they're all on a wave,
Making a splash that only the brave!

So if you find laughter when waves meet the shore,
Just know it's a dance, who could ask for more?
Sway to the rhythm, let happiness swell,
In this watery world, all is well!

## Undercurrents of Memory's Flow

Fish tell tales of sunken delight,
Mermaids giggle, they're quite the sight.
Octopus juggling with eight clumsy limbs,
Doesn't quite notice when wiggles and swims!

Anchors drop slowly, they take a bow,
While dolphins leap high, hey look at me now!
Seahorses chuckle, they ride the tide,
Their tiny little steeds fill hearts with pride.

Sandcastles topple, much to our glee,
When an unexpected wave shouts, "Now you see!"
Coconuts splatter with bright pineapple sails,
The tropics above tell the funniest tales!

So let's dive in deep, where laughter won't quit,
With these playful wonders, we'll surely commit!
The underwater giggles are always a blast,
In this watery realm, life's fun everlast!

## Ballet of the Moonlit Tide

Ballet shoes crabs wear with flair quite divine,
Twirl under moonlight, they dance on a line.
Squid in tuxedos dive into the sway,
Making quite the splash, what a grand display!

Clownfish giggle, well-known for their pranks,
Joining the mermaids, they all share their thanks.
Turtles spin circles, they never get dizzy,
While plankton's doing the tango—not busy!

The driftwood orchestra begins their sweet tunes,
As waves tap their toes beneath silver moons.
Barnacles tap dance, their grip is so tight,
While starfish sing praises of this wondrous night!

So if you find yourself near salty shores,
Join in the ballet, hear the ocean's roars!
Laugh with the critters, swirl with the tide,
In this moonlit dance, let your joy be your guide!

## Lullabies of the Water's Edge

Ocean's embrace hums a sleepy song,
While snoozing seals nap, it won't be long.
Crabs in their beds, tucked up safe and sound,
Dream of sushi treats, oh what have they found!

Waves cradle shells, with a gentle hum,
Singing soft melodies, come one, come all!
Starfish count sheep in the twilight glow,
Resting up for their ballet show.

Seagulls yawn widely, fluffing their feathers,
While fish play peek-a-boo, swimming like leathers.
Kelp waves sway softly, it's a lullaby tease,
In the charming waters, life's a cozy breeze!

So nestle in close, feel the calmness blend,
With the ocean's soft whispers, let laughter ascend.
Dream of adventures, both silly and grand,
Tomorrow brings fun to each wave-kissed strand!

## A Splash of Hidden Harmonies

The fish are in a conga line,
They wiggle and they shine.
A crab in shades does sashay by,
With a wink and a playful sigh.

The octopus wears a top hat bold,
His dance moves are a sight to behold.
Jellyfish twirl in a bubble ballet,
Laughing as they drift away.

Starfish clap with all their might,
In the deep, they groove all night.
A dolphin takes a comical spin,
In the splash, let the fun begin!

Underwater, the party swells,
With sounds of laughter, ocean bells.
So next time you dip your toes,
Remember the show that no one knows!

## **Tidal Troupe of Whispers**

High tide brings the merriest crew,
A seahorse with a tutu too.
They chatter and twirl with glee,
What a sight beneath the sea!

Octopi play a game of charades,
While sea turtles throw parades.
A clam cracks jokes, oh what a treat,
While starfish tap dance with their feet.

Scallops shimmy in pairs, oh so sweet,
As a school of fish keep the beat.
They've got moves you won't believe,
In the ocean, there's no reprieve!

Bubbles burst with every cheer,
As creatures dance without fear.
So if you think the ocean's grand,
Join the funny wave at hand!

## The Dance of Hidden Depths

Deep in the blue, hilarity lurks,
With dolphins doing quirky quirks.
A clownfish juggles seashells bright,
Under the moon, what a sight!

The anglerfish pulls a goofy face,
While flounders flop, just in case.
A crab plays tag with seaweed strands,
You wouldn't think this was their plans!

Anemones wave in excitement too,
With a wink and a swirl just for you.
Beneath the surface, laughter's the key,
In water's embrace, we all feel free!

So dive down low, take a chance,
Join the waves in a silly dance.
Where secrets spin in every turn,
In the depths, the ocean does yearn!

**Beneath the Silken Surface**

Bubbles whisper, tales unfold,
As fish whoop it up, brave and bold.
With floppy fins and silly grins,
Their shenanigans just begins!

A pufferfish tries to impress,
With a dance that's anyone's guess.
Seahorses twirl in airy holds,
While snails groove at their own bolds.

Waves crash softly, splashes cheer,
A sea cucumber joins the sphere.
With each little shimmy and sway,
They turn the tide in a comical way!

So if you think it's quiet down there,
Remember the laughter, the fun, the flair.
Under the surface where joys resound,
The charm of the sea knows no bound!

## Beneath the Waves' Embrace

A fish in a tux, oh what a sight,
He twirls and he swirls under moonlight.
With jellyfish waltzing, all in a row,
They throw quite a party, just thought you should know.

A crab plays the drums, cranking the beat,
While octopuses jam with flippers and feet.
The seaweed's a dancer, all frizzled and green,
They've got moves, oh my, like you've never seen!

But wait, what's that? A shark in a hat!
He's doing the cha-cha, imagine that!
With guppies as backup, all flailing about,
They rock 'n' roll under, without any doubt!

So if you dive deep, don't be afraid,
Just join the party, it's a grand parade.
Underwater laughter, in bubbles and glee,
Join in the fun, come dance with the sea!

## Secrets in the Current

A mermaid sits grinning, her hair in a mess,
She's tangled in seaweed, oh what a dress!
The dolphins are giggling, flippered delight,
As they spin 'round her tail, what a whimsical sight!

With clamshells as trumpets, the concert begins,
The shrimp tap their feet, rhythmically spins.
A seahorse DJ spins tunes without end,
Each beat just a ripple, oh what a blend!

The deep has its secrets, in bubbles they chatter,
As sardines swim by, tails all a-flatter.
The secret's revealed in a bubbly burst,
A dance-off beneath, oh they're quenching their thirst!

So glide through the currents, just take a small peek,
At the shenanigans happening, oh what a freak!
Under water's surface, where laughter resounds,
The current's a stage, with silliness abound!

## **Ripples of Enigma**

A walrus in shades, lounging with flair,
He throws back a drink in his comfy chair.
With seals on the dance floor, shaking their tails,
They're grooving and moving, wearing huge veils!

The ripples are winks, like whispers on air,
While fish pass the gossip with nibbles to share.
A turtle in sneakers, he's pounding along,
But his slow-motion shuffle plays all the wrong songs!

A crab with a top hat, he's got style and grace,
He's leading the conga, taking up space.
As anemones sway to the beats from above,
They smile at the fun, oh they're filled with love!

So dive into this riddle, let giggles abound,
In the world below, joy is easily found.
With ripples and chuckles, each wave sings a tune,
In this underwater circus, beneath the sun's moon!

## Ballet of the Salted Breeze

There's a pelican prancing, with a flair for the arts,
He's leaping and lunging, winning all hearts.
With sandpipers tapping, they tap on the shore,
They're all putting on quite a whimsical score!

Seagulls in tights, oh what a scene,
They pirouette perfectly, all shiny and clean.
The tide's a conductor, waving waves as the beat,
While crabs kick their legs, rhythmically neat!

Starfish are clapping, they shine like the stars,
While dolphins do flips, showing off who they are.
The salty breeze tickles, gives giggles galore,
In this ballet of misfits, who could ask for more?

So join in the frolic, let laughter take flight,
Under the sun's gaze, dreams sparkle and light.
In a splendid diversion, where silliness reigns,
The dance of the day, with no room for chains!

## The Subaqueous Soirée

Bubbles rise, a fish disco,
They twirl and swirl, moving to and fro.
Crabs in tuxedos, oh what a sight,
Dancing with seaweed beneath the moonlight.

Starfish snapping selfies, all in good cheer,
Their limbs in the limelight, they spread no fear.
A clownfish giggles, a jellyfish jives,
Underwater shindig where everyone thrives.

Snorkelers stumble upon this grand bash,
With fins and tails making quite the splash.
Laughter echoes in waves all around,
In this underwater realm, joy knows no bound.

As currents carry tales of fun-filled delight,
The seabed's revelry lasts all night.
With sea cucumbers swooping down for a glance,
Join the frolic, you too can dance!

# Secrets of the Water's Embrace

Gossip flows with the tide, it's true,
A dolphin's wit sharp, quick as a crew.
Octopus whispers, "Who wore it best?"
Seashells clench pearls, all in jest.

Mermaids lose their combs, oh what a pisser,
Their hair a mess, but they're still a blisser.
Treasure chest jingles with tales of mishaps,
A crab telling jokes, everyone claps.

Sand castles crumble, they all laugh aloud,
While starfish giggle, all huddled and proud.
Nautilus grins, with secrets to tell,
Diving deep down, they're under a spell.

So swim by the waves where stories unfold,
With laughter and quirks, pure joy to behold.
In depths of blue, quirky mysteries arise,
Underwater hijinks wear a sassy disguise!

## Sway of the Coral's Heart

In the rhythm of reefs, fish shimmy and sway,
Coral branches tap dance, adding to the play.
Anemones chuckle, puffing out their cheeks,
While stingrays glide, pulling off funny squeaks.

Turtles twist, vintage vibes in their shells,
Bubbles popping, like little laughter bells.
A parrotfish chuckles, a joke in its smile,
Bringing joy to the current, mile after mile.

Clownfish in socks, the fashion's delight,
Distracting the angelfish, giggles in sight.
Currents swirl laughter, a festival boasts,
Underwater antics, a party for ghosts.

So dance with the tides—no time to be shy,
Join the coral cavort, let your troubles fly.
In this bubbly world where joy knows no end,
With fins and fins together, laughter's the trend!

## Ebb and Flow of Enigmas

What's lurking in depths? The hermit crab grins,
His shell is a fortress, but he invites friends.
With riddles to share, they gather around,
Fathoms of laughter in waves unbound.

Seaweed waltzes, a green ball of fun,
No one knows where it's been, but it's on the run.
Pufferfish giggles, inflating with pride,
A bobble of humor, they glide with the tide.

The tides bring tales, of mischief and play,
Old bottle messages washing away.
Seagulls squawk jokes, while fish roll their eyes,
In this underwater maze, humor never dies.

As the sun sets high, the ocean turns gold,
With smiles as bright as the stories retold.
So, dip your toes in this world of glee,
Where every wave whispers, "Come laugh with me!"

## The Enchanted Seafoam Nocturne

In the moonlight, waves do prance,
Seafoam bubbles in a dance.
Starfish giggle, crabs tap their feet,
As fish parade down the watery street.

Mermaids toss their hair with glee,
While dolphins dive with a splashy spree.
A jellyfish jumps in a silly twist,
Calling out to the clams, 'Don't you get the gist?'

Seagulls squawk with a comedic flair,
Landing too close to the octopus lair.
Tangled tentacles, the uproar grows,
Laughter echoes where the tide flows.

So come, my friends, join this seaside jest,
In the surf's embrace, we'll find the best.
With every wave, a fresh surprise,
Under the starlit, dancing skies.

## **Celestial Ribbons in Saltwater**

Swirling colors, a painter's brush,
The sea giggles, creating a hush.
Whales sing out in a playful key,
As pirates argue over the last cup of tea.

Barnacles build their clammy fort,
While sea cucumbers hold a court.
Crabs in tuxedos, looking quite sly,
Waltz with the stingrays as they fly by.

A shoal of fish performs a ballet,
While octopuses knit in their own way.
With bubbles blowing, and laughter so bright,
The tides tickle toes every night.

Join the fun in this watery bay,
Where whimsy dances, come what may.
For in the depths, the antics abound,
In this salty realm where joy is found.

## Voices Carrying Beneath the Surface

Whispers rise from the salt-stirred depths,
Turtles gossip with their slow, wise breaths.
Clownfish joke in a bubbly scene,
While sand dollars spin like a merry machine.

Eels make faces, what a sight to see!
Playing peek-a-boo just like you and me.
Puffer fish puff, trying to frighten,
But they end up just giggling and lightenin'.

Crabs don hats from driftwood detritus,
Having a tea party, oh what a riot!
Seashells whisper secrets, one by one,
Of the silly deeds from the fishes' fun.

So plunge in deep, join the chatter and cheer,
For underwater antics are always near.
With every dive, laughter you'll find,
In the watery realm where joy's intertwined.

## Mysteries of the Sublime Current

Currents swirl with a humorous twist,
Questions bubble up, 'What have we missed?'
Fish play hide and seek in the kelp,
Making mischief, just like a helper.

Squirrels dive from the sandy banks,
Chasing shells with their playful pranks.
Starfish hold contests of who can cling,
To the rocks while the sea urchins sing.

A walrus slips on a slick seaweed mat,
Rolling and laughing, 'Oh, how fancy that!'
Coral reefs hum tunes so absurd,
While sea horses sashay, looking quite stirred.

Join in the ruckus, don't be afraid,
In the currents of laughter, memories are made.
With salty breezes and chortles galore,
Life in the tide is never a bore.

## Serenade of the Seafoam

The jellyfish waltzed in a gown of blue,
While shrimp held a ball, who knew they'd break through?

A crab tried to tango, a little too fast,
But he slipped on a clam and fell with a blast.

Starfish sang loudly with voices quite rare,
They formed a boy band, but no one would care.
The waves rolled in laughter, a jubilant cheer,
As dolphins joined in, their flips full of cheer.

Each wave brought a chuckle, a ticklish tease,
While seagulls squawked loudly, a cacophony of ease.
A turtle did limbo, under the tide,
The ocean's got moves that can't be denied!

So if you hear giggles when tides start to play,
Know it's just the sea's way to brighten your day!
A narrative timeless, in bubble and foam,
The ocean's just jiving, calling us home.

## Echoes from the Abyss

Deep down in the depths where the weird creatures dwell,

The octopus jives, spinning tales none can tell.
A fish in a bowtie asked, "What's the best jam?"
The grouper replied, "Let's call it a clam!"

Bubbles, they giggle, as deep waters flow,
With mermaids all gossiping, stealing the show.
A pufferfish danced with the flair of a beau,
Till he puffed up in fright, stealing the glow!

Ghostly eels wiggled, with shimmering skins,
They played hide and seek, wiggling for wins.
A whale told a story, the best of the day,
But half of it vanished when the sea stole away!

So if you should wander where shadows make fun,
Listen close to the echoes, the laughter's begun!
The deep's got the humor, a curious blend,
Keep searching the depths, there's joy 'round the bend!

# Choreography of the Nautical Night

At twilight the sea begins its grand show,
With crabs doing ballet, and the fishes in tow.
The squids bring the rhythm, pulsating with style,
While sea turtles glide, with grace that's worthwhile.

A plankton parade twinkled so bright,
They danced in the moonlight, a truly wild sight.
The sea cucumbers tossed in a jig,
Though no one could tell if they danced or just swigged!

With each crashing wave, the choreography swells,
A chorus of laughter, the best kind of spells.
The starfish applauded with five little hands,
And dolphins all hummed to the beat of the bands.

So when stars begin twinkling, and the night sets in,
Know that the ocean's got a party to sin!
It's a wacky gala, that no one should miss,
Join in the fun, give a splash and a twist!

## Mysteries Beneath the Surf

What lies beneath surface, in shadows and glee?
A clam with a secret shared a drink with a bee.
The sand dollars giggled; they know what's to come,
A treasure map drawn to the sound of a drum.

A fish wearing glasses read under the blue,
"Shhh, it's a mystery, don't let it squeak through!"
An octopus whispered, "Let's spice up the tale,
I'll bring the popcorn, and we'll never fail!"

The conch shell revealed the stories so grand,
From shipwrecks to mermaids with treasure so planned.
And crabs with their spectacles noted with flair,
"Why did the starfish not play hide and seek?

Because he couldn't find any feet, oh so rare!"
With chuckles and splashes, the night gently spun,
Each wave brought a secret, a riddle, a pun.
So dip in your toes, take a chance, hear the laughs,
For beneath all the surf, are the ocean's own gaffs!

www.ingramcontent.com/pod-product-compliance
Lightning Source LLC
Chambersburg PA
CBHW062113280426
43661CB00086B/573